GRETA GARBO

A Hollywood Portrait

GRETA GARBO

A Hollywood Portrait

Marie Cahill

SMITHMARK

This edition published in 1992
by SMITHMARK Publishers Inc.,
112 Madison Avenue,
New York, New York 10016.

SMITHMARK books are available for bulk purchase for sales promotion and premium use. For details write or telephone the Manager of Special Sales, SMITHMARK Publishers Inc., 112 Madison Avenue, New York, NY 10016. (212) 532-6600.

Produced by Brompton Books Corp.,
15 Sherwood Place
Greenwich, CT 06830.

ISBN 0-8317-4603-3

Printed in Hong Kong

10 9 8 7 6 5 4 3 2 1

All photos courtesy of American Graphic Systems Archives.

Page 1: Her career in Hollywood ended when she was only 36, but the Garbo mystique continued to fascinate the public.
Page 2: Garbo, as Sweden's Queen Christina, a woman very much like herself.
Facing page: Garbo's haunting beauty was only part of her allure.

INTRODUCTION

Of all the stars who have ever captured the imagination of film lovers, none has projected the magnetism of Greta Garbo. She was called 'The Divine,' the 'dream princess of eternity,' 'the Sarah Bernhardt of films.' Surrounded by an aura of mystery, Garbo was a star who appealed to both men and women. Able to portray any sort of role, she played characters who were sensual and pure, suffering and hopeful, world-weary and life-inspiring.

Born Greta Louisa Gustafsson on 18 September 1905 in Stockholm, Sweden, she grew up in poverty and went to work at 13 when her father died. Her first job was as a lather girl in a barber shop. While working as salesgirl in a

Facing page: A Clarence Bull portrait of Garbo for **Ninotchka** (1939).

Below: After arriving in Hollywood, Garbo immediately became a star of silent films.

department store, she appeared in a promotional film for the store entitled **How Not to Dress** (1921). After a second promotional film, this one for a bakery, she tried her hand at slapstick, as the female lead in **Peter the Tramp** (1922).

By this time, Garbo was intrigued by acting and applied for and won a scholarship to the Royal Dramatic Theatre training school. During her training for the stage, she was discovered by director Mauritz Stiller, one of the great directors of Sweden's golden age of film. He cast her in the epic **Gösta Berling's Saga** (1924, also known as **The Legend of Gösta Berling**, **The Atonement of Gösta Berling** and **The Story of Gösta Berling**), and she immediately attracted the attention of film critics across Europe.

Stiller became her mentor: he coached her, brought her into his social circle and managed all her personal affairs. The two of them were referred to as Pygmalion and Galatea, Beauty and the Beast or Svengali and Trilby.

In 1924, Louis B Mayer of MGM offered Stiller a job in Hollywood. He accepted, on the condition that Garbo be included in the offer. Mayer agreed somewhat reluctantly, not realizing he had found hidden treasure. When she arrived in Hollywood, studio publicity was at a loss as how to promote the new star. Her quiet ways finally provided the key, and MGM introduced the 'Swedish Sphinx.'

When Mayer saw the daily rushes for Garbo's first US film, **The Torrent** (1926), he finally saw that Garbo could mesmerize an audience. Even before filming was completed, he revised her contract, giving her a higher salary. When the film was released, critics concurred with his assessment and the Garbo legend was born.

Garbo's next film, **The Temptress** (1926), found her working with her former mentor, but their roles had changed. Garbo was the star, while Stiller failed to receive the recognition that had been his in Sweden. He found himself constantly at odds with Mayer and was fired from the film before its completion. Stiller turned to Paramount, but fared no better there, returning to Sweden, ill and depressed. Legend has it that he begged Garbo to return with him, and she refused, but was plagued by guilt for years for leaving him in his hour of need.

Flesh and the Devil (1927), her third American film, only served to reinforce the Garbo mystique. The electric charge between Garbo and costar John Gilbert was clearly more than two people devoted to their craft. When they were paired again in **Love** (1927), MGM fueled the rumors with their coy advertisements of 'Garbo and Gilbert in **Love**.' Garbo, however, wasn't talking and ended their affair in 1929. Over the years, Garbo's name was romantically linked with several men, including director Rouben Mamoulian, conductor Leopold Stokowski and nutrition expert Gaylord Houser, but rumors were never substantiated and she remained single.

MGM devoted an enormous amount of time and energy to building the Garbo mystique. She was assigned the best directors, the best screenwriters and the best cameramen. The sets were lavish, the costumes elegant. The publicity department pulled out all the stops. With her first talkie,

Anna Christie (1930), ads boldly proclaimed 'Garbo Talks!' and for **Ninotchka** (1939), her first comedy, it was 'Garbo Laughs!' In 1935, the New York Film Critics named her best actress for her performance in **Anna Karenina**, an honor bestowed again in 1937 for **Camille**. She never won an Academy Award, although in 1954 she did receive a special Oscar 'for her unforgettable screen performances.'

Offscreen, Garbo remained aloof and mysterious. True to her image, she guarded her personal life from the public and the press. The more reclusive she became, the more the public desired. Her early retirement from film in 1941, at the height of her career, only enhanced her aura of mystery. Until her death on Easter Sunday in 1990, she lived the life of a recluse, dividing her time between Switzerland, the Riviera and New York City. Though seldom in the public eye she remained in the public's mind, a woman of beauty and mystery, always a legend.

Above, left and right: Garbo played the vamp to perfection.

GRETA GARBO

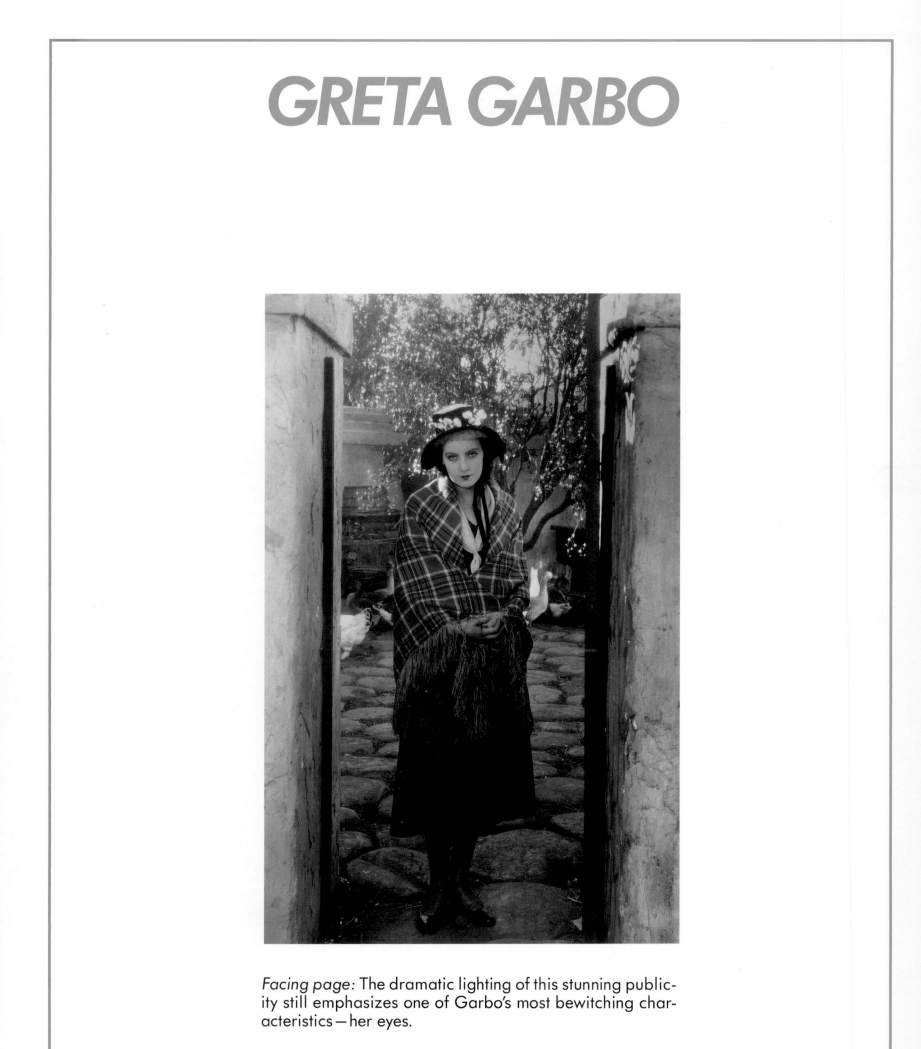

Facing page: The dramatic lighting of this stunning publicity still emphasizes one of Garbo's most bewitching characteristics—her eyes.

Above: Greta Garbo made her American debut in MGM's **The Torrent** (1926) opposite Ricardo Cortez. She was hailed as the find of the year, and Laurence Reid in *Motion Picture* declared 'She is not so much an actress as she is endowed with individuality and magnetism.' The Garbo myth had begun.

MG74527

Above: Garbo's second film for MGM was **The Temptress** (1926). Once again, the critics adored her, citing her allure and magnetism. A comparison of Garbo as the Temptress with Garbo as the innocent young Spanish girl in **The Torrent** *(see page 10)* illustrates her chameleon-like ability to transform herself completely. With just the flutter of an eyelash or the subtle raising of an eyebrow, she could convey a mood.

The still *on the facing page* shows Garbo with Antonio Moreno, who played her lover. This was the only film they starred in together. Mauritz Stiller, her Swedish mentor, was assigned to direct the film, but conflicts with the studio resulted in his replacement by Fred Niblo.

These pages: At first, MGM publicity didn't know what to make of the quiet Swedish girl. Naturally shy, she resented their efforts to thrust her into the public eye.

The original plan was to promote her as the All-American outdoorsy type, but once Garbo was behind the camera a distinct persona emerged, not at all the sporty type. In her early roles in silent films, Garbo mesmerized audiences with her beauty and passion. She was unique, and it didn't take the studio long to realize they had discovered gold.

65-237

Above: **Flesh and the Devil** (1927) marked Garbo's first appearance with John Gilbert, her lover onscreen as well as off. Thrilled by their torrid love scenes on screen, the fans were wild with delight to learn of their offscreen romance.

MGM took every advantage of the situation and immediately paired them in the silent version of Leo Tolstoy's novel *Anna Karenina*, called **Love**, with Garbo as Anna and Gilbert as Vronsky, the military man she loves. The studio coyly promoted the film with the slogan 'Garbo and Gilbert in **Love**' (1929).

While filming **Love**, Garbo and Gilbert made plans to elope, but as they neared the Justice of the Peace, Garbo sought refuge in a ladies' room and then boarded the next train home.

Above: Garbo and Gilbert shared equal billing for **Flesh and the Devil**, though by no means did they share equal status. Gilbert had succeeded Rudolph Valentino as the screen's 'Great Lover' and was one of Hollywood's highest paid male stars. Eventually their positions would be reversed, for Gilbert would be unable to make a successful transition from silent films to talkies.

Above: A rather stiff looking publicity still of Greta Garbo and Conrad Nagel for **The Mysterious Lady** (1928). According to Antoni Gronowicz's unauthorized memoir of Garbo, her two costars in **The Mysterious Lady**—Conrad Nagel and Gustav von Seyffertitz—fought over her and were prepared to duel in the name of honor.

Facing page: A secluded garden provided the perfect place for a lover's tryst in **The Mysterious Lady**. The photography was the handiwork of William Daniels, Garbo's friend and colleague. Fred Niblo directed this film about a beautiful Russian spy (Garbo) who kills her spymaster in order to save her enemy lover.

Above: More than any other movie star, Greta Garbo epitomizes Hollywood's Golden Age.

Facing page: A spy story, **The Mysterious Lady** teamed Garbo with Conrad Nagel, one of the leading romantic stars of the era.

380-103

Above: **A Woman of Affairs** (1929) was Garbo's first contemporary role. Playing a doomed flapper, she was again paired with John Gilbert. The film was based on Michael Arlen's scandalous novel, *The Green Hat*.

Above: Greta Garbo was more than beautiful; she had a transcendent presence.

353-95

353-4-1

Wild Orchids (1929), a lush romantic drama, cast Greta Garbo as Lillie Sterling, a young woman bound for the Orient with her husband. Nils Asther (*facing page and above*) played a Javanese prince, a man of great mystery and charm. He attempts to seduce Lillie, but as a proper married woman she slaps him. Later, however, she will succumb to his advances.

While filming the love scene with Nils Asther, Garbo received word that Mauritz Stiller had died in Sweden. She collapsed when she heard the news.

Overleaf: In the end, Lillie is reconciled with her husband, played by Lewis Stone, whom Garbo described as 'a man of beautiful character.'

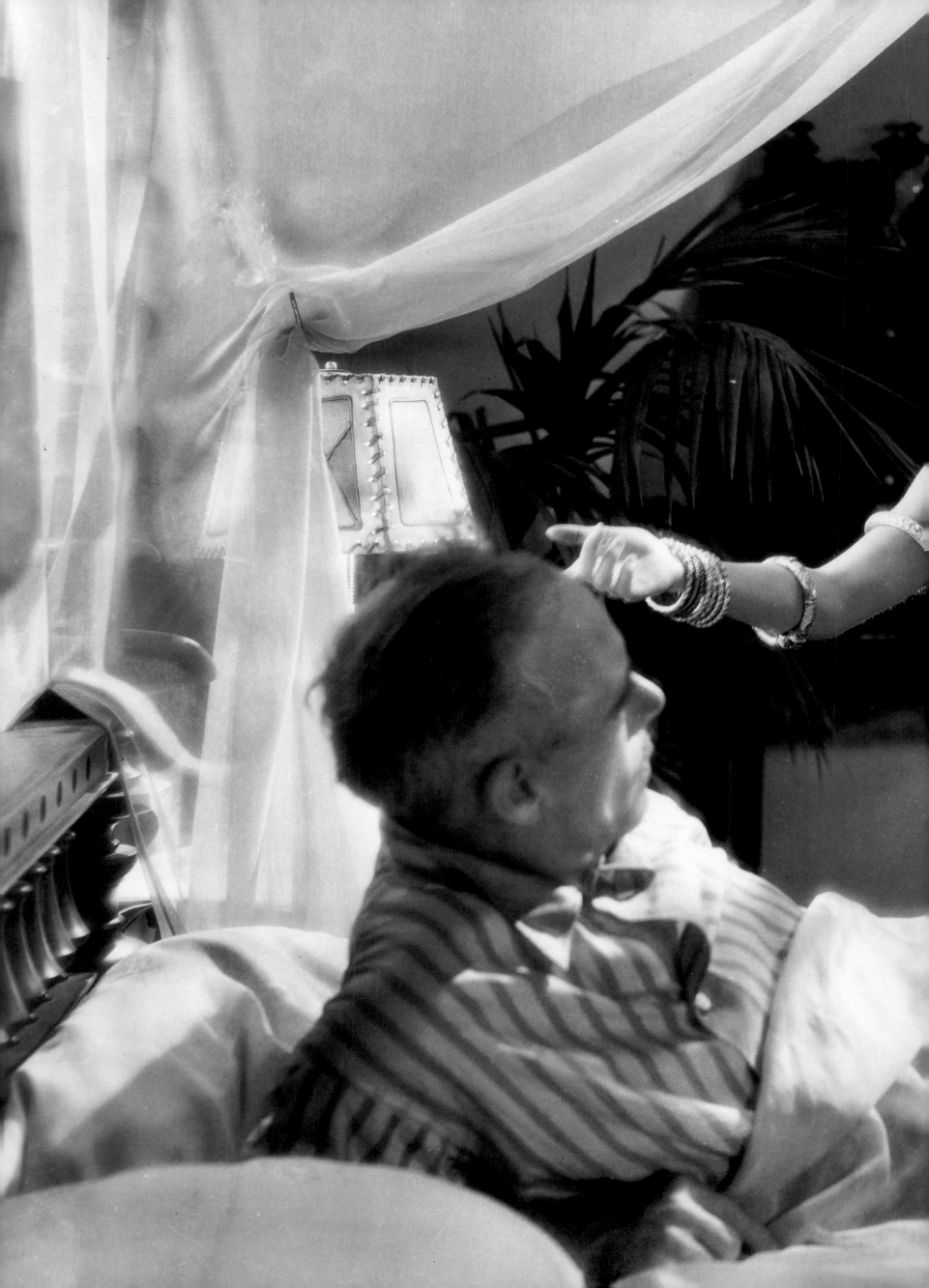

Left: After **Wild Orchids,** Garbo again starred opposite Nils Asther in **The Single Standard** (1929). Another native of Sweden, Asther—like his leading lady—had been discovered by Mauritz Stiller. A suave and romantic star, he was very popular during the final years of silent films, but with the advent of sound, his accent limited his appeal.

In **The Single Standard**, Garbo played Arden Stuart, a San Francisco debutante and 'New Woman,' while Asther played Packy Cannon, a sailor-artist. The two go off together on Packy's yacht, but she returns to San Francisco on her own. Finding herself alone in the world, Arden marries Tommy Hewlett (John Mack Brown) who has always loved her. When Packy returns to San Francisco, Arden finds herself still attracted to him.

While the film began with the premise that women can be as sexually active as men, **The Single Standard** took the safe approach and concluded with the Garbo character choosing home and hearth over her former lover. An earlier Garbo film would likely have concluded with Arden leaving her husband and child for Packy, but studio heads were reacting to public outcry over the various sexual scandals, such as the notorious Fatty Arbuckle case, that shocked Hollywood in the early 1920s. In 1930, the Hays Office Production Code would impose rigorous standards on what could and could not be seen on the screen. While acknowledging that adultery is sometimes essential to the plot, the Hays Office decreed that adultery 'must not be explicitly treated, or justified, or presented attractively.'

While on location on Catalina Island, Garbo learned that John Gilbert, her great love, had married Ina Claire, a Broadway actress. The press immediately began hounding Garbo for her reaction to Gilbert's marriage. She withdrew from the public, and as the years went by, she became more and more guarded in her dealings with the press.

Above: All of Garbo's films were love stories, and children seldom figured in them.

Facing page: Garbo in a costume for **The Single Standard** by Adrian. As chief costume designer for MGM, Gilbert Adrian helped glamorize the likes of Norma Shearer, Jean Harlow and Joan Crawford, but no one inspired him like Garbo, and when she retired from films, he soon followed.

Left: In **The Kiss** (1929), Greta Garbo played Irene Guarry, the wife of a silk merchant. Pierre, the son of her husband's business partner, falls in love with Irene. Although she resists his advances, her husband in a fit of jealousy attempts to kill the young man. Instead, Irene kills him with his own gun as she tries to defend Pierre.

She is accused of murder and the case goes to trial, with Irene defended by her former lover André (Conrad Nagel). She is acquitted and the two go off together, though he does not yet know the true circumstances of her husband's death. Greta Garbo and Conrad Nagel had previously starred together in **The Mysterious Lady**.

Overleaf: Filming a scene from **The Kiss**, Garbo's tenth film for MGM. **The Kiss** was directed by Jacques Feyder and photographed by William Daniels.

Right: Conrad Nagel confronts Greta Garbo before agreeing to take her case in **The Kiss**.

Garbo has often been called an 'interior' or 'reflective' actress. This film was unusual for Garbo because it was more action-oriented. We see Garbo intervening in the struggle between her husband and her young admirer. First on her knees, she lunges toward her husband and kills him.

Overleaf: A scene from **The Kiss**. The last silent film made at MGM, **The Kiss** signalled the official end of the silent era. Garbo could no longer delay entering the world of sound. Her next film would be a talkie.

Above: 'Gimme a viskey, chincher ale on the side and don't be stingy, baybee' were the first words uttered on the screen by Greta Garbo in the film version of Eugene O'Neill's **Anna Christie** (1930). MGM selected this film for Garbo's sound debut because the title character is Swedish and would therefore have an accent like Garbo's.

'Her voice,' wrote Richard Watts Jr of the *New York Herald Tribune* 'is revealed as a deep, husky, throaty contralto that possesses every bit of that fabulous poetic glamour that has made this distant Swedish lady the outstanding actress of the motion picture world.'

Anna Christie was an artistic triumph and a commercial success. Critics, audiences and studio executives alike were enthralled with Garbo's performance, which earned her a nomination for an Academy Award. Garbo, unlike so many stars of silent films, made the transition to talkies with style and grace.

Facing page: Garbo with George F Marion, as the father who deserted Anna when she was a child.

Above: Charles Bickford played the sailor who finally won the heart of the man-hating Anna.

Garbo's original contract with MGM had no provision for talkies. Though it was standard procedure to sign a talk agreement, Garbo had declined because of her lack of confidence in her English language skills. The death of the silent film made her reconsider her position. Louis B Mayer eased the transition for her by promising that she could do a version of **Anna Christie** in German, a language she was more comfortable with, if she would do the English version first. In those days, films were neither dubbed nor subtitled. Rather, a number of versions in various languages were prepared for distribution in foreign markets.

Above: Greta Garbo with Marie Dressler. Originally a vaudeville and musical comedy star, Marie Dressler received critical acclaim for her performance as Marty in **Anna Christie**, a serious part that went against her usual casting. Garbo was so impressed with Dressler's performance that she sent her a bouquet of yellow chrysanthemums. The two women became close friends.

Overleaf: Director Clarence Brown (in chair) guides Garbo through her first talkie. One of MGM's top directors, Brown was often teamed with Greta Garbo, for he knew how to bring out the best in the temperamental star. Brown directed Garbo in two silent films — **Flesh and the Devil** and **A Woman of Affairs** — and five talkies — **Anna Christie, Romance, Inspiration, Anna Karenina** and **Conquest**.

These pages: The part of Rita Cavallini, an opera diva in
Romance (1930), called for a lavish wardrobe.

Right: Garbo in her second talkie, **Romance** (1930). As MGM's crown jewel, Greta Garbo received the best the studio had to offer: the best directors, set designers, costumes and so on. **Romance** once again found Garbo under the skillful direction of Clarence Brown and the camerawork of William Daniels. Daniels, one of the most brilliant cinematographers in the history of American film, was assigned to most of her films. He was, in fact, known as 'Garbo's cameraman' throughout the 1930s. In addition to capturing her luminescent beauty on film, he was able to win her trust and accorded her with preferential treatment, insisting that her scenes be shot on closed sets with only essential personnel allowed.

Overleaf: **Romance** is the story of a worldly opera diva and an innocent rector. Gordon Gavin played the part of the rector who falls in love with Rita (Greta Garbo) but ultimately refuses to succumb to temptation.

Above: **Romance** also featured Lewis Stone. A star on Broadway and the silent screen, Stone was 50 by the time sound revolutionized Hollywood. He continued to enjoy great success at MGM as a mature leading man, starring in close to 200 films all told. Garbo admired Stone immensely and appeared with him in seven films, which is the most often she costarred with any one actor.

Facing page: Greta Garbo and **Romance** costar Gordon Gavin.

Overleaf: This scene still from **Romance** illustrates the mesmerizing effect Garbo had on screen.

These pages: After **Romance**, Garbo did **Inspiration** (1931), another film featuring Clarence Brown's direction and William Daniels' photography. Garbo played an artist's model who falls in love with a diplomat. Her past threatens to damage his career, so she leaves him rather than ruin his aspirations. As a woman willing to sacrifice her happiness for the sake of her lover, Garbo gave a stunning performance. The part of her lover, André, was played by Robert Montgomery.

Overleaf: Garbo, with Beryl Mercer in **Inspiration**.

GRETA GARBO - Metro Goldwyn - Mayer

MG-13541

These pages: Publicity stills for **Inspiration**. As part of her contract with MGM, Garbo would pose for publicity stills on one day only, which meant that Clarence Bull had to photograph all changes in costume and hairstyling in that single day.

These pages: **Susan Lenox: Her Fall and Rise** (1931) paired Garbo with Clark Gable, who was on his way to becoming one of Hollywood's most dashing leading men. Directed by Robert Z Leonard, the film was a typical early 1930s melodrama that had Garbo searching the jungles of South America for her true love (Clark Gable).

British film censors banned **Susan Lenox** because it was based on a 'scandalous' novel by David Graham Phillips. The censors later relented after 125 feet was cut from the film and the title changed to **The Rise of Helga**, so as not to be associated with Phillips' novel.

These pages: Working with the great Garbo signalled that Clark Gable had achieved star status. Garbo, however, found Gable's acting wooden, and he was no fonder of her. Garbo did not enjoy making the film, and believed that only William Daniel's creative camerawork saved the film from being a total disaster.

These pages: One of the most famous sequences from **Mata Hari** (1931) in which Garbo, in an exotic costume, dances suggestively around a huge idol.

Above: **Mata Hari** was based on the life of the Javanese-Dutch spy for the German Secret Service during World War I. Before filming began, British censors declared that the execution of the glamorous spy must not appear on the screen. What the censors hadn't anticipated was the scene on the *facing page*, which suggests that Mata Hari had a stronger influence over Lt Alexis Rosanoff (Ramon Navorro) than did the Virgin Mary. Irving Thalberg, chief of production at MGM, offered to film a retake with a portrait of Alexis' mother instead of the Virgin Mary, but the censors couldn't agree on how the mother should be dressed in the photo. Surprisingly, they did agree to permit the portion of the execution scene to which the dialogue refers.

These pages: Garbo as Mata Hari, the world's most famous vamp. Garbo's costumes for the part were as exotic as the part itself.

MG-15

These pages: One of Garbo's best known roles is the ballerina in MGM's star-studded production of **Grand Hotel** (1932), in which she murmured the immortal line, 'I want to be alone.'

Overleaf: Garbo willingly yielded to John Barrymore's request that their love scenes be filmed with his left profile showing.

These pages: Based on the play by Luigi Pirandello, the plot of **As You Desire Me** (1932) revolves around a woman suffering from amnesia, with Garbo alternating from a slinky, blonde cabaret singer to the wife of a count.

Though she had read Pirandello extensively and was a great admirer of his philosophy, Garbo found the role of Zara difficult and felt that her presentation of the character lacked depth.

Garbo and her leading men in **As You Desire Me**: Erich von Stroheim (*above*) as Salter, the novelist who had a hypnotic influence over her, and Melvyn Douglas (*facing page*) as her husband, Count Varelli.

Right: Zara/Maria (Greta Garbo) is united with her husband, Count Varelli (Melvyn Douglas). She is not certain of her true identity, but she has fallen in love with Varelli and wants to be his wife.

One critic declared 'the love scene between Douglas and Garbo are the high points of the film, and they are almost equal the ones played so long ago by Gilbert and Garbo.'

As You Desire Me was one of Melvyn Douglas' first films. His debonair manner and good looks would soon make him one of Hollywood's most popular stars of the 1930s and early 1940s. Frequently paired with some of Hollywood's most glamorous leading ladies—Joan Crawford, Marlene Dietrich, Myrna Loy—he starred opposite Garbo in **Ninotchka** (1939), her only comedy, and **Two-Faced Woman** (1941), her final film.

Above: As the blonde Zara, Garbo has a harsher, more angular look than we have seen before.

Facing page: With Erich von Stroheim. The complete personality change of the woman in **As You Desire Me** has been likened to the change that Garbo herself underwent from shopgirl to living legend.

Overleaf: Zara (Garbo) discovers a clue to her true identity.

These pages: Swedish royalty. Garbo in male garb (*above*), as Queen Christina of Sweden travels incognita to meet the Spanish Ambassador, Don Antonio (John Gilbert). **Queen Christina** (1933) was the first sound film starring the once torrid combination of Greta Garbo and John Gilbert. Gilbert's career had declined with the advent of sound, and legend has it that Garbo arranged for her former lover to be her costar. Garbo's assistance was to no avail. Gilbert made only one more film before he died of a heart attack and alcoholism.

These pages: Garbo felt more comfortable in the role of the Swedish monarch than she did in any other part. The film was directed by Rouben Mamoulian, who, unlike many directors, was able to achieve a close rapport with the enigmatic actress.

These pages: As always, Garbo's eyes speak what words cannot say, revealing the emotional turmoil of the strong-minded queen.

GRETA GARBO   Metro-Goldwyn-Mayer

776X115

Facing page: Like Queen Christina, Garbo would choose
a path of self-exile.

Above: Garbo's next film was **The Painted Veil** (1934), a
film noted for Garbo's unique headgear.

These pages: Basec on the novel by W Somerset Maughm,
The Painted Veil involved a love triangle. George Brent
played the part of Garbo's lover.

Facing page: A Clarence Bull portrait of Garbo as Tolstoy's tragic heroine, Anna Karenina.

Above: This shot of Garbo rehearsing the mazurka for **Anna Karenina** (1935) was taken by William Grimes from the catwalks. Director Clarence Brown is in the foreground, pointing to Garbo.

Overleaf: After a vacation in Sweden, Garbo reported for work on **Camille** (1937), the film adaptation of Alexander Dumas' *La Dame aux Camélias*, the tale of a Parisian courtesan who dies of tuberculosis. Garbo is seen here with Lionel Barrymore, who played the father of her true love, Armand.

Above: On the set of **Camille**, Garbo confers with camera-man Hal Rossen, who was temporarily filling in for the absent Bill Daniels. The film was completed by Karl Freund.

Facing page: The part of Dumas' immortal courtesan had been played by the world's most illustrious actresses, but none could compare to Garbo's interpretation of Marguerite Gautier. For her performance in **Camille**, Garbo received a nomination for an Academy Award, the *Litteris et Artibus* award from the King of Sweden, the best actress award from the New York Film Critics and a raise from MGM.

Overleaf: Garbo in **Conquest** (1937), a fictionalized account of Napoleon Bonaparte's mistress, Countess Marie Walewska (Greta Garbo). The part of Napoleon was played by Charles Boyer. In Britain, the film was exhibited as **Marie Walewska**.

'Garbo laughs,' MGM announced when Garbo appeared in her first comedy — **Ninotchka** (1939). Sig Rumann, Felix Blessart and Alexander Granach (*above*) played the three missing Soviet commissars Garbo was sent to Paris to find. While in Paris, she falls in love with a count (Melvyn Douglas).

Proving that she had the sense of humor to spoof her own humorless legend, Garbo gave an intelligent and truly funny performance, which earned her another nomination for an Academy Award. One critic declared, 'It is a joyous, subtly shaded and utterly enchanting portrayal which she creates, to illuminate a rather slight satire and make it the year's most captivating screen comedy.'

Above: **Ninotchka** also featured Bela Lugosi in his first (and only) comedic role as Commissar Razinin. Director Ernst Lubitsch scored one of the biggest hits of his career with the satirical script written by Charles Brackett, Billy Wilder and Walter Reisch (and half a dozen uncredited writers).

The film was remade as **Comrade X** in 1940 and **The Iron Petticoat** in 1956, and Cole Porter used the story as the basis for the Broadway musical **Silk Stockings**.

Above: MGM promoted the **Two-Faced Woman** as the new Garbo, with bobbed hair and a daring wardrobe. The new Garbo was versatile too—she could swim, ski and dance the chicachoca rhumba. MGM's publicity could not save **Two-Faced Woman**. Critics panned the film and the Catholic Church's Legion of Decency condemned it. Garbo turned her back on Hollywood, never returning to the dream factory.

Facing page: Though neither of them knew it at the time, Clarence Bull and Greta Garbo, one of his favorite subjects, would never meet again to work their magic behind the camera. This portrait was made during their last session on 3 October 1941.

Above: Garbo meets with the press to discuss her proposed comeback. The project, however, was not to her liking. The answer was no, and so it would remain.

Facing page, above: The air of mystery that had always surrounded Greta Garbo was heightened when she retired from filmmaking. She became a recluse, but her desire to be left alone went unheeded, her privacy violated by the click of a *paparazzo's* camera as she walked along. On occasion, however, she would greet the camera as an old friend, and as this portrait (*facing page, below*) reveals, Garbo, in retirement, had lost none of her allure.

Filmography

How Not to Wear Clothes (1921, Swedish advertising short)
Peter the Tramp (1922, Swedish Silent)
Gösta Berling's Saga (1924, Swedish Silent)
The Street of Sorrow (1925, Swedish Silent)
The Torrent (1926, Silent)
The Temptress (1926, Silent)
Flesh and the Devil (1926, Silent)
Love (1927, Silent)
The Divine Woman (1928, Silent)
The Mysterious Lady (1928, Silent)
A Woman of Affairs (1929, Silent)
Wild Orchids (1929, Silent)
The Single Standard (1929, Silent)
The Kiss (1929, Silent)

Anna Christie (1930)
Romance (1930)
Inspiration (1931)
Susan Lenox: Her Fall and Rise (1931)
Mata Hari (1931)
Grand Hotel (1932)
As You Desire Me (1932)
Queen Christina (1933)
The Painted Veil (1934)
Anna Karenina (1935)
Camille (1937)
Conquest (1937)
Ninotchka (1939)
Two-Faced Woman (1941)

Index

Academy Award 9, 40, 100, 104
Adrian, Gilbert 30
Anna Christie 9, 40-43, 40-45
Anna Karenina 9, 16, 43, 96-97, 97
Arlen, Michael 22
Asther, Nils 24-25, 25, 29
As You Desire Me 76-82, 76-85
Barrymore, John 72, 73-74
Barrymore, Lionel 97, 98-99
Bickford, Charles 42, 42
Blessart, Felix 104, 104
Boyer, Charles 100
Brackett, Charles 105
Brent, George 94-95, 95
Brown, Clarence 43, 44-45, 48, 56, 97, 97
Bull, Clarence 6, 61, 97, 106
Camille 9, 97, 98-99, 100, 100-101
Claire, Ina 29
Conquest 100, 101-102
Cortez, Ricardo 10
Crawford, Joan 30, 80
Daniels, William 19, 33, 48, 56, 64, 100
Dietrich, Marlene 80
Douglas, Melvyn 78, 79, 80, 80-81, 104
Dressler, Marie 43, 43
Dumas, Alexander 97, 100
Feyder, Jacques 33
Flesh and the Devil 8, 16-17, 16-17, 43
Freund, Karl 100
Gable, Clark 62-65, 63-64
Gavin, Gordon 48, 49-50, 52, 53
Gilbert, John 8, 16-17, 16-17, 2, 8, 86
Gösta Berling's Saga 8

Granach, Alexander 104, 104
Grand Hotel 72, 72-75
Green Hat, The 22
Grimes, William 97
Harlow, Jean 30
Hays Office 29
Houser, Gaylord 8
How Not to Dress 8
Inspiration 43, 56-61, 56-61
Kiss, The 32-39, 33, 36
La Dame aux Camélias 97
Legion of Decency 106
Leonard, Robert Z 63
Litteris et Artibus 100
Love 8, 16
Loy, Myrna 80
Lubitsch, Ernst 105
Lugosi, Bela 105, 105
Mamoulian, Rouben 8, 89
Marie Walewska 100, 101-102
Marion, George F 40, 41
Mata Hari 66-70, 66-71
Mayer, Louis B 8, 42
Mercer, Beryl 56, 58-59
MGM 8, 10, 16, 36, 43, 68, 100, 104, 106
Moreno, Antonio 12, 13
Motion Picture 10
Mysterious Lady, The 18-20, 19-20, 33
Nagel, Conrad 18-19, 19, 32-37
Navarro, Ramon 68, 69
New York Film Critics 9, 100
Niblo, Fred 13, 19
Ninotchka 9, 7, 80, 104, 104-105

O'Neill, Eugene 40
Painted Veil, The 93-95, 93-95
Paramount 8,
Peter the Tramp 8
Phillips, David Graham 63
Pirandello, Luigi 76
Queen Christina 2, 86-93, 86-93
Reid, Laurence 10
Reisch, Walter 105
Rise of Helga, The 63
Romance 43, 47-55, 48-53, 56
Rossen, Hal 100, 100
Royal Dramatic Theatre 8
Rumann, Sig 104, 104
Shearer, Norma 30
Single Standard, The 28-31, 29-30
Stiller, Mauritz 8, 13, 25, 29
Stone, Lewis 25, 26-27, 53, 53
Stokowski, Leopold 8
Susan Lenox: Her Fall and Rise 62-65, 63-65, 110
Temptress, The 8, 12-13, 13
Thalberg, Irving 68
Tolstoy, Leo 16, 97
Torrent, The 8, 10, 10, 13
Two-Faced Woman 80, 106, 106
Von Stroheim, Erich 79, 79, 82, 83
Watts, Richard Jr 40
Wilder, Billy 105
Wild Orchids 24-27, 25, 29
Woman of Affairs, A 22, 22, 43

Page 110: As Susan Lenox, Garbo was filled with longing for her lost love.

Page 112: Every role she played was imbued with the Garbo mystique.